Kermit Save
the Sw

D0118916

By Richard Chevat
Illustrated by Tom Leigh

A MUPPET PRESS/GOLDEN PRESS BOOK

It was a bright summer morning, and Kermit was getting ready for a trip.

"Hey, Kermit, where are you headed?" asked Fozzie Bear, who was passing by.

"I'm going to visit some old friends back in the swamp," Kermit explained. "I haven't been there in a long time, and I really miss the place."

"You do?" Fozzie was surprised. "Gee, Kermit. What's so great about a swamp?"

"Why don't you come along and see?" said Kermit.

"Me? Come along with you? Great!" cried Fozzie, and he ran home to pack a bag.

Soon they were driving through the countryside, heading for Kermit's swamp.

"What's it like in a swamp?" asked Fozzie. "I've always been too *bogged down* to visit one! Get it? *Bog? Bogged down?*"

"It's wonderful," said Kermit. "The trees are tall and shady, the moss is cool and green, and there are beautiful water lilies everywhere."

"Wow," said Fozzie. "And I thought a swamp was just full of icky old mud."

"Mud? That's the best part," Kermit said with a happy sigh. "And we're almost there!"

"Hey, what's that thing?" asked Fozzie as they turned onto a dirt road.

In front of them stood a large billboard.

"'Swamp World'?" Kermit read out loud. "I wonder what that's all about."

Kermit and Fozzie headed on down the road toward the swamp.

"Look! It's the beaver pond," said Kermit. "And there's old Fergus!" He pointed to a beaver sitting on a log by the side of the pond.

"Hi, Kermit!" said Fergus. "Back for a visit?"

"That's right," Kermit replied. "I'm showing my friend Fozzie the swamp."

Fergus nodded. "You're just in time," he said. "Pretty soon there won't be a swamp to show."

"What?" Kermit cried. "What do you mean?"

"Well," said Fergus, "a few weeks ago this fellow came around and said he wanted to build a big shopping mall and amusement park here."

"Swamp World!" said Fozzie.

"That's right," Fergus replied. "So we got together and decided it might be a good idea. We're signing the deal next week."

"You think it's a good idea?" asked Kermit.

"Why not?" Fergus answered. "We'll all get free rides in the amusement park. I hear they're building a great water slide."

"But what about your dam?" Kermit asked.

"Won't need a dam," Fergus answered. "They're draining all the water."

Just then a musical voice called out,
"Kermit! Welcome home!"

"It's Lulu the mockingbird!" said Kermit.
"Lulu, what's all this about draining the swamp?"

"Yes, isn't it exciting?" Lulu answered.

"But I don't understand," said Kermit.
"Why do you want to give up this beautiful place?"

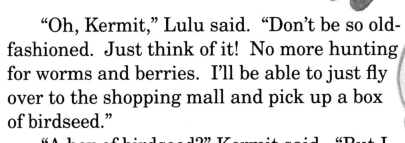

"Oh, Kermit," Lulu said. "Don't be so old-fashioned. Just think of it! No more hunting for worms and berries. I'll be able to just fly over to the shopping mall and pick up a box of birdseed."

"A box of birdseed?" Kermit said. "But I used to love hearing you sing when you gathered food each day."

"Oh, I won't have to sing anymore, either," said Lulu as she flew away. "There will be music at the mall!"

"Music at the mall?" Kermit moaned. "Fozzie, this is terrible. We've got to find my cousin Nemo. I bet *he* doesn't want the swamp to be drained."

Nemo was sitting under a tree, holding a brand-new pair of roller skates.

"Hi, Kermit!" Nemo called out when he saw them coming. "Boy, am I glad to see you. I've got a problem!"

"I knew that's how you'd feel!" Kermit cried.

"I need someone to teach me how to
roller-skate," Nemo explained. "I want to be
ready when they put in the new sidewalks."

"*Sidewalks?*" shouted Kermit. "Who needs
sidewalks in a swamp?"

"Golly, Kermit," said Nemo. "You can't
roller-skate on mud!"

Kermit shook his head sadly. "I guess nobody cares about this place but me," he said, sighing.

"It's too bad—but at least you got here in time to say good-bye to it," Fozzie said, trying to cheer Kermit up.

Suddenly Kermit's face brightened. "Fozzie, that gives me an idea!" he cried.

That night Kermit invited his friends to a
big party under the tree by Fergus's pond.
Almost everyone in the swamp was there—
Fergus, Lulu, Nemo, Alice the alligator,
Tennyson the turtle, and Garnett the raccoon
and her children.

"Gee, thanks for throwing this great party,
Kermit," said Nemo as he munched on popcorn.

"Glad you like it," Kermit said. "Because this isn't any old party. This is a good-bye party."

"Who's leaving?" Lulu asked.

"Why, lots of things," said Kermit. "Like this old tree. All the trees will have to be cut down to make room for the mall."

"But where will we build our nests?" asked Lulu, her voice suddenly growing hoarse.

"And this pond," Kermit added. "We'd
better say good-bye to it, too."

"Now that I think about it, I *would* miss
this place," Fergus said, his eyes misting over.

"Where would I go?" Alice the alligator
asked. "I swim here."

"Not only do I swim here," Tennyson the turtle
chimed in, "I love to chew on the swamp grass."

"Well, better say good-bye to the grass," said Kermit. "It'll be paved over. And the water lilies, too—"

"And the mud! I just remembered how much I like to play in the mud!" Nemo cried.

"Gee, we get a lot more from this swamp than I realized," said Lulu.

"Not just us," Nemo said. "The flowers, the bugs . . . everyone needs it."

"Even I'm starting to like it," Fozzie said sadly.

"Well, there's just one thing to do," Fergus said in his loud, growly voice. "Tell them we don't want Swamp World here after all!"

"He's right!" Lulu sang out. "What do you say, everyone?"

"Keep the swamp!" the crowd began to shout.
"Yay!" cried Kermit.

"Kermit, you did it!" said Fozzie as everyone cheered. "You saved the swamp. But I still feel bad about one thing."

"What's that?" Kermit asked.

"I really like amusement parks," Fozzie replied. "Well, Fozzie," Kermit answered, "look at it this way. There are lots of amusement parks. But a good swamp is hard to find!"